BLACK WIDOW SPIDER

CONTENTS

WHAT IS A LIFE CYCLE?

All animals, plants and humans go through different stages of their life as they grow and change. This is called a life cycle.

Baby ➤ Child ➤ Adult

GROSS LIFE CYCLES

All life cycles are different. They can be quick or slow. They can have lots of steps or not many at all. Life cycles can also be gross and full of scary sounds and smelly splats.

WHAT IS A BLACK WIDOW SPIDER?

A black widow spider is an arachnid, which is a type of animal with eight legs. Just like other spiders, black widow spiders can be found sitting on a web.

ack widow spiders have a scary, gross life cycle.
here is a lot of biting, chewing and churning. It has
horrible ending too...

7

EGG CASES

A black widow spider starts its life cycle as an egg. Spider eggs are laid by adult female spiders. Female spiders have a red mark on their bodies.

female black widow will lay hundreds of eggs at the
ame time. She then wraps them in a case made of
ilk to keep them safe. Silk is made inside the spider's
ody, and it can also be used to make webs.

SPIDERLINGS

Baby spiders will soon hatch, meaning they come out of the eggs. After they hatch, they will break out of the egg case. Baby spiders are called spiderlings, and there can be hundreds in every egg case.

When the spiderlings hatch, they are so hungry that they often eat their own brothers and sisters! Not many survive to become an adult. How gross!

A STICKY SITUATION

It's time to find a new home. The spiderlings shoot out a sticky blob of silk. The silk carries the spiderling in the wind to its next home. This is called ballooning.

When it is ready, the spiderling will make its first web. The web is made of very sticky silk and is often very messy. Lots of insects can get trapped in it. The spider will then eat those insects.

MEALTIME

When the black widow spider has grown into an adult, it looks for a mate. Mates are two animals of the same kind that can make babies together. For spiders, there needs to be one female mate and one male mate.

Once the female black widow has mated with the male, she may do something horrible. She may gobble him up! This helps the eggs to grow inside the female.

END OF THE ROAD

When she is ready, the female black widow will lay her eggs. This starts the life cycle all over again.

Black widow spiders often live for around one year.
However, some black widow spiders may live for up
to three years.

A GROSS LIFE

Black widow spiders do other gross things too. They have fangs, which are long, sharp teeth. They can use their fangs to bite other animals, including humans.

When a black widow spider bites something, it passes venom through its fangs. That venom can make us very ill. Never touch a black widow spider!

A black widow bite can make our bodies ache and hurt. A bite might also make it difficult to breathe.

Don't worry, a black widow spider will not bite you if you keep away from it. Black widow spiders only bite when they are scared! Don't touch one, just in case.

GROSS LIFE CYCLE
OF A
BLACK WIDOW SPIDER

1 A female black widow lays eggs.

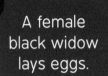

2 Spiderlings hatch and eat each other.

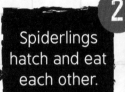

3 Spiderlings make their webs and catch food.

4 Adult black widows mate and the female may eat the male.

GET EXPLORING!

There are lots of different types of spider. When you go outside, see how many spider webs you can find. Make sure you do not touch any of the webs!

QUESTIONS

 1 What colour is the mark on a female black widow spider's body?

 2 What are eggs wrapped in?
a) Leaves
b) Dirt
c) Silk

 3 What is ballooning?

 4 What is step 2 in the life cycle of a black widow spider?

 5 What can you do to stay safe from a black widow spider?